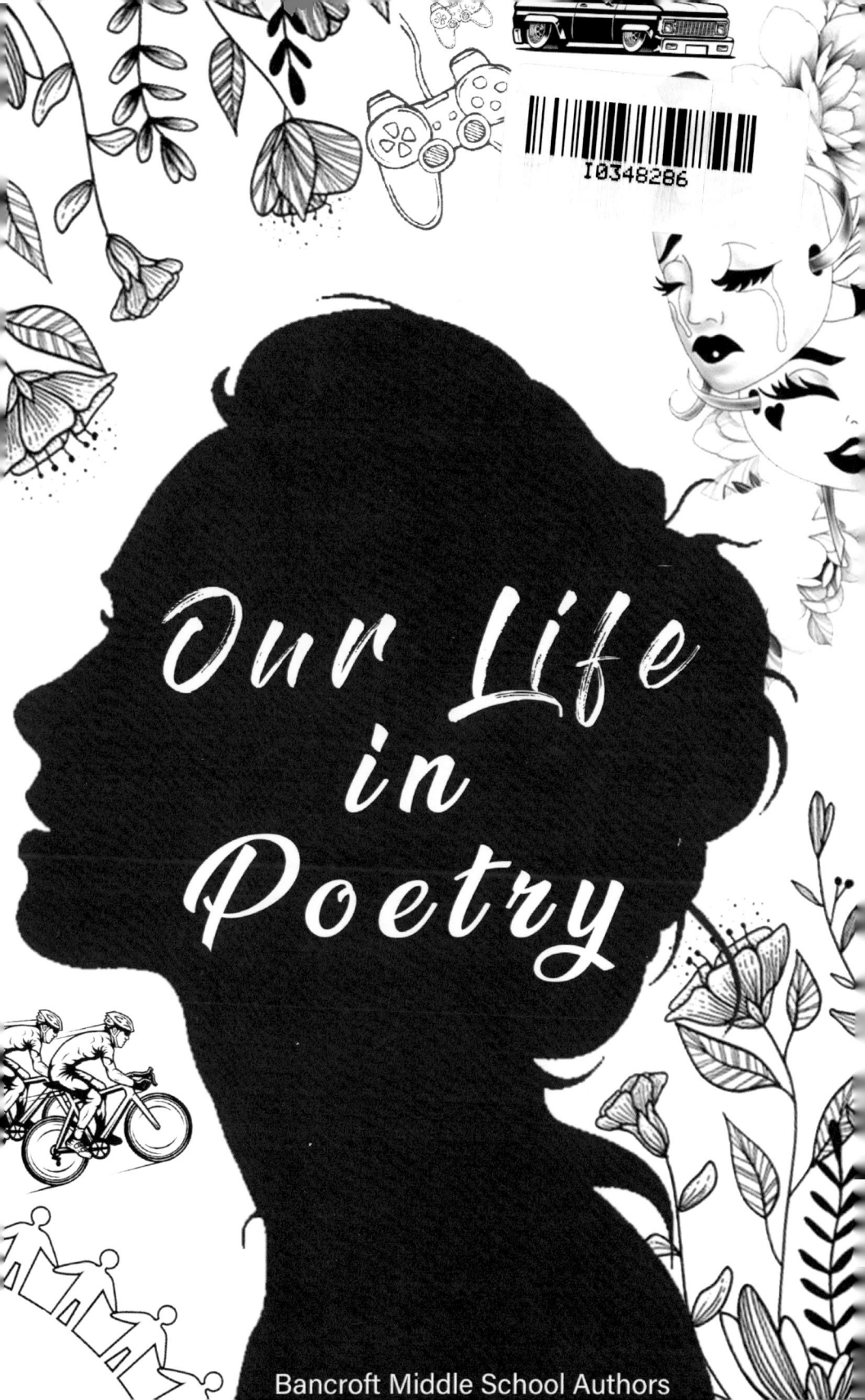

Our Life in Poetry

Copyright © 2024 Bancroft Middle School

All rights reserved.

Published by Red Penguin Books

Bellerose Village, New York

ISBN 978-1-63777-613-1

No part of this book may be reproduced in any form or by any electronic or mechanical means, including information storage and retrieval systems, without written permission from the authors, except for the use of brief quotations in a book review.
All individual works are copyrighted to the writers and artists.

Dear Readers,

Mx. Hirsh and Ms. Mali are proud to congratulate the student poets and artists of Bancroft Middle School in their wonderful accomplishment of creating an anthology that speaks from the heart. Searching for a way to share the passion and creativity that the scholars embody, Mx. Hirsh encouraged them to shoot for the stars and " Our Life in Poetry" was born; a project that had to be shared beyond the walls of the classroom.
 Inspired by the scholar's dedication and voice, this work is proudly offered as a glimpse into our amazing scholars and their lives.

As it always goes, things are best said in the words of our youth:

" Do you like learning about student's lives? Have you ever wondered what they are going through or their passions? This book isn't like any other book you have read, it is written by Bancroft Bruins! Our College, Career and Readiness community took great effort and dedication going through many drafts, asking for feedback and even hiring a professional editor to put this masterpiece together. Our poetry book titled, " Our Life In Poetry" is a collection of themes such as cooking, biking, shopping, gaming and family dynamics that bring to light lessons that we have learned. We had the pleasure of collaborating with the amazing art scholars, we shared our poems and discussed illustrations together. The artwork adds a level of creativity and expression that makes the reading experience even more enjoyable. We are happy to share our book and we hope that you will enjoy the experience of reading it."

Sincerely,
3rd Period CCR, 2024

Dear Dad,

You work every day to put a roof over our head.

You teach us how to defend ourselves.
You make some of the best foods.
  From the shrimp you make
   to the roasted chicken.
   The flavors feel like home.

You only take a day off from work.
I wish you could work less.
  So I could spend more quality time with you.

You are a great dad
Because you are hardworking.
You take care of us.
You buy the things we want and need.
  The basketball hoop
   because you know it's my favorite.
You are funny and strong.
You are a wonderful dad.

You taught us things we didn't know.
You've been with us
All our life.
I love how you support us.
You are my hero.

Andrew Vallejo

At First

I didn't like my dad's musical taste.
It sounded like forks
scratchin' on a plate.
It was just not my vibe.
He would play that music
all the time:
in the car,
in the house,
in the shower…

I thought it was as cringey
as an awkward conversation
with your doctor.
I didn't like it,
but later on
when I was older,
I just got used to it.

Song after song,
the vibe started to
match my mood.
In my free time,
I would listen to his playlist.
I started singing, dancing,
and even wrote my own.

I then found songs like
"Last Kiss" by Pearl Jam
and "Anoche Me Enamore" by Ana Polo y Los Apson
and shared them with my dad.

Now we vibe together.

Josue Martinez-Marin

Soccer Rule #1

In soccer you have to

        be *prepared* at all times.

You need to know what

        position you are playing.

You need to have a *connection*

        with your **teammates**.

You have to play

        with **pressure** on your back.

Some teammates will be

        selfish and take your goal.

No matter how bad you are,

keep a good

        mindset inside of you.

Kevin Guerrero-Magdaleno

Creative

Relating
or revealing natural
creative skill…

As in, I like to draw
Fundamental Paper Education characters
whenever I am bored
or I just want to draw in general.
I sometimes draw in school,
when I'm in the car,
or when I wait to be picked up.
Calmness like notes of music.

As in, when I wait to be picked up,
I'm inspired by the songs in the album
"Basics in Behavior,"
relaxing and creating

with my brother,
then falling asleep,
which means more energy for tomorrow
to get things done faster.

As in, art can help me calm down
when I am angry and upset.
It's nice to get all the stress out
of myself, chilling and trying not to
let my frustration take control whenever
I'm accused of doing something.

Even though I didn't do it
and get the blame for it,
I take a deep breath
and do what calms me down.
Also, I do not get mad at someone who annoys me
and gets me in trouble, but I still watch what I do.

Victoria Davila Viramontes

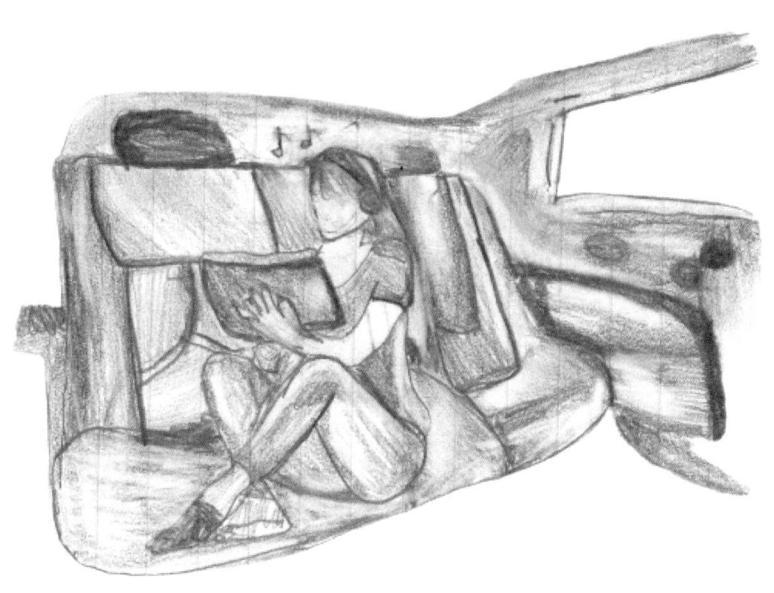

At First

I didn't like
going to friends' houses
and seeing their parents:
two, two, two...
Every time I counted,
it never changed.

On the way home,
I'd glance at my mom
in the driver's seat:
the brightness of hazel eyes
through the mirror
embraced in the warmth
that shed off her body
like the most perfect day of spring.

Swept up in her love,
all aches of jealousy
melted away
like a popsicle
in the heat of July.

At first I didn't like
how different my family looked.
But now I know
I am the lucky one—
the one who
never starved for love,
the one who
had a connection so strong
nothing could tear it down.

My mom,
my rock,
my everything…
How grateful I am for
you.

Gabriel Hirsh

☾ Cooking Rule #1★

-˙`★˙- ＊˚₊*☾＊˚₊* -˙`★˙-

Rule number one:
The kitchen is made for your creativity.
It's ok if you don't make it look good. ★
It's not always about looks.

.˚✲˚̣̣̥=̲☆·˚☆

People may judge,
but that's
how people are.

.˚✲˚̣̣̥=̲☆·˚☆

You'll improve yourself, **so do NOT give up** ★

.˚✲˚̣̣̥=̲☆·˚☆

Cooking will turn from a flaw into a flawless
hobby for you,
but not everybody makes flawless food.

.˚✲˚̣̣̥=̲☆·˚☆

Refrain from burning the food.
Don't turn the heat too high or too low! ★
You don't want it raw,
but you don't want it burnt.

.˚✲˚̣̣̥=̲☆·˚☆

Don't drop the food: it will make a mess.
But that's ok if you do! You are still learning.

.˚✲˚̣̣̥=̲☆·˚☆

You don't have to rush.
Go at the pace
you want to go.

.˚✲˚̣̣̥=̲☆·˚☆

Don't get upset with people's opinions.
They are helping. ★
"It's too raw!" or "it's too salty."
Both will help you improve your past mistakes.

.˚✲˚̣̣̥=̲☆·˚☆

Be happy with
what you have made
even if it's not the best.
Only some people are experienced chefs.
But that is alright
if you are still you when cooking. ★

Michelle Bounnay

At First

At first,
I didn't like my elective.
I wanted Music class, not Art.
I was disappointed.

At home,
my mom gave me a blank stare,
As she asked, " Did you get in?"
"No," I replied with saddened eyes.

At school,
I decided to tell the counselor
and gave him my reason,
I was better at Saxophone
so he switched me into Music.

I was joyful,
humming to myself
while walking back home.

At home,
I had a smile on my face
and Mom immediately noticed,
so I told her what happened.
She was elated
as she grinned at me.

Jethro De Guzman

Makeup Rule #1

I like makeup.
It's fun,
but you have to make sure

to find the right foundation shade.
You don't want to look

too light or too dark,
or too orange.

Makeup is like art,
to express ideas.
but you can't just add
any type of makeup to your face.
Eyeshadow, eyeliner, lipstick,
all ways to show your true colors.

Makeup can also make you break out,
so you have to find the right products.

If you have an oily skin type,
you need to use matte and oil-free products.
If you have dry skin type,
you need to use a more hydrating product
so your skin doesn't peel.

Make-up is for everyone,
show your confidence
feel free.

Meleny Toledo

MAKEUP RULES

Shopping Rule #1

At the
    M
      A
        L
          L
You must try on everything
Not too small
Not too
    B
      A
        G
          G
            Y
Don't spend too much time in one store
Don't spend all your money
Go shopping in different stores
Go to different **MALLS**
Be willing to explore

Try on bodysuits
Try on swimsuits
Try on shorts
Try on shirts
Go
    S
      H
        O
          P
            P
              I
                N
                  G
Have a girls' day
Spend time with yourself

Even if you don't have **MONEY**
You can window shop
And see what you can buy later
"It's just shopping"
But it's important to me
It's a way to express who I am

Marilyn Rojas

At First

I did not want a little sister.
I was used to being the favorite child.
I *hated* having to share.
I *hated* having to let her
play with my toys,
my money,
my phone...
I never wanted to share a room.

She would always complain,
saying "it's dirty."
She would always get me in trouble,
she would always come when I went out,
she always came to my friend's house like my shadow.

I never thought
she would grow on me.
Then I did...
She started to be nice for once,
but she also started to steal from me.

She took stuff my dad gave me.
She even broke my favorite toy once,
The military soldiers of different color greens.

I hated that she did that,
but I had to forgive her.
She is my sister
at the end of the day.

Then we started to play together more
and she stopped stealing from me.
And now, conversations flow.

Lorenzo Herrera Mendoza

At First

I didn't like my haircut.
It was as bad as failing a math test.
What was I thinking?
What was wrong with me?
My friends made fun of me.

My hair was too short;
I didn't recognize myself.

In my seventh-grade year,
I changed my hair.
I went to the barber
and got a low taper.
It was slowly improving
but still not what I envisioned.

It was way too short;
I didn't like it.

Eighth grade was better.
OMG!
My hair…
It was so good,
so I felt better.
I loved it more
and my friends did too.

Joel Melena

Fortnite Rule #1

Some friends can take
your good guns, loot, or health.

My friends don't help me,
but they like to steal my weapons.

And they don't care about me,
but they yell at me when I don't help them.
Fighting with enemies,
Leaving me to heal
Getting in trouble for grades at school.

Just like in life, some people don't help you,
but you still help them

and they don't care about you,
yet you care about them

but that's how   l

                      i

                              f

                                  e

                                        i

                                            s

William Rodriguez

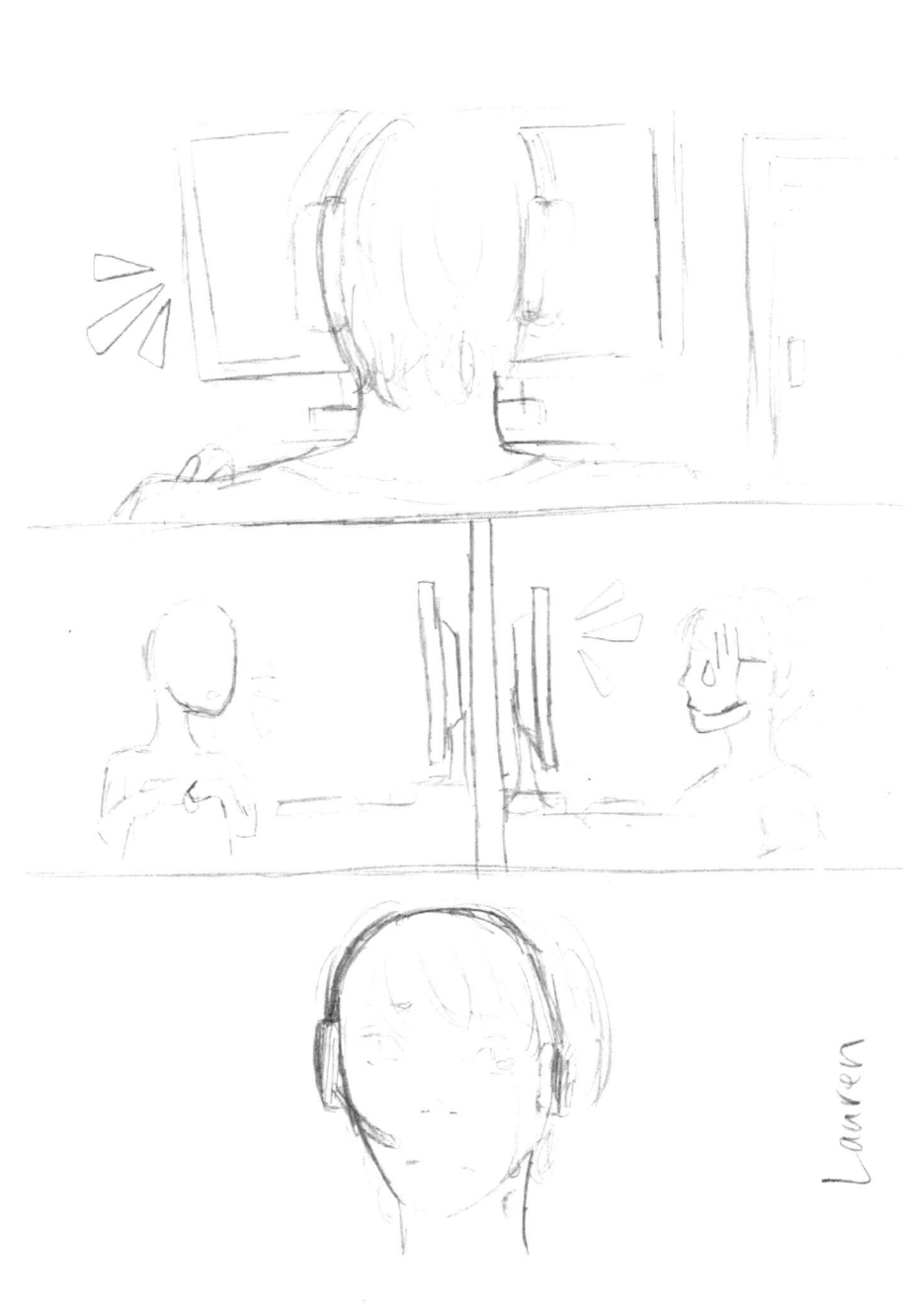

Five Nights at Freddy's (FNaF) Rule #1

In this game,
you have to survive
until 6 am,
BUT there are animatronics stopping you,
so you have to use doors and cams.

There are other ones like FNaF 2, 3, 4,
sister location, Ultimate Custom Night (UCN),
fan games, security breach, ruin.

I liked this game when I was 9 or 10 years old.
It made me want to watch a series of games.

I could be a night guard
while looking at cams.
I didn't let anyone break in,
and I could roam around
like I was in the game.

Max Lopez

Fortnite Rule #1

In Fortnite you must box yourself up
so the haters don't get to you.
You have to protect
your team and get them back up
if they get down.

Just like in life,
people will try to get you down
they can feel depressed,
but you can help them.
And in life,
you must not let them
get to your head.

Ignore the negativity
like you are
escaping the pump.
The bullet is like haters
protect yourself from them.

Your team might not share
the loot with you,
but you have to share it with them
or they go ballistic
and leave you.

Be kind,
be a good teammate,
and no matter what the case,
be the last squad standing.

Alex Paz

THIS GAME SUCKS!

NO WAY! MY FIRST VICTORY ROYALE

Bike Rule # 1

When I am on the bike,
I don't have any worries.
It feels like the sound of waves
calming me down.

And I can ride my bike as long as I want,
and I love when the wind hits my face
because I just feel free.

Like in life,
just live your life freely
with no worries.
If you fall off your bike,
just get back up.

I like listening to music
when I am on my bike
because it feels like I'm flying
on a cloud.

Music can change your mood.
It can make you happy
if you are sad in life.
Don't let what
other people say get in your head.

Free yourself from the stress.

Michael Becerra

Dear Kindergarten Friend,

      I always wanted to tell you a lot
          You have always been there for me
            You cared about me
You taught me
how to play soccer
and kick the ball high
            And I have cared about you too
              You have been my best friend
since kindergarten
              I have continually seen how you treat your other friends
                And tell them beautiful things about themselves
              " you are the best"
              " you are close to me like a sister"

              And some of my favorite things
you have done are
                teach me how to kick the ball high

        and loved me
as a best friend
since kindergarten

And your laugh sounded like
a mouse squeaking
and it always got me so bad

Since kindergarten
you helped me with homework
on call, answering questions together.
Whenever something bad happened
you talked to me

I respect you so much

              and I am glad that I met you

You helped me
whenever I needed it

        I have loved you

   so much Jesse Alexander Venegas
I have loved you a lot
since kindergarten

Lexi Luna

At First

At first, I didn't like Fortnite.
I thought it was a game that everyone played,
but nobody told me how bad it was.
I thought it was a game that when I played,
it would be good; it's just that I had to stare at my phone,
and it was harder for me.

I found out about Fortnite when I was with my cousins.
I asked about the game they were playing,
and they told me, so I started playing
and ended up enjoying it.
It was really good, I guess,
but I was braggy when we won the battle pass.
I actually really liked it,
but I stopped playing for a while,
and after a month, I began playing again.
I won the game and was very happy,
and in some time,
I got really good at Fortnite.

Jairo Castillo

Family Problem

Bad family
Or unstable family.
  T
    U
      M
        U
          L
            T
              U
                O
                  U
                    S
                      Family.

As in, I was happy or silly
Or playing around with my friends.
Funny, friendly, supportive
    F
      R
        I
          E
            N
              D
                S

But I had to drive three hours to see
My tio because he was in the hospital.
He fell off a ladder on two glass tables.

As in, I wasn't seeing my brother for a while
Because my brother is in jail
And I can't see him
'Cause I'm too young to see him.
He went to jail because he had a patrol officer,
And he kept doing things he can't do
Like have a gun and steal cars.

Stephanie Garcia

Hiking Rule Number One

is an easy rule to follow.
You should always know what to do
when you hike up a tall hill

or a mountain or a trail
through the woods.

You should always make sure
to keep a steady pace

so you don't get too tired
or dehydrated
while still challenging yourself enough.

Don't go home without a
                  W
                    O
                      R
                        K
                out
OR without finding the peace
during a nice walk up a hill
like Jack and Jill.

Jack fell and Jill ran down,
forgetting to conserve their energy
and thus forgetting the first rule
of HIKING.

Fernando Beiza

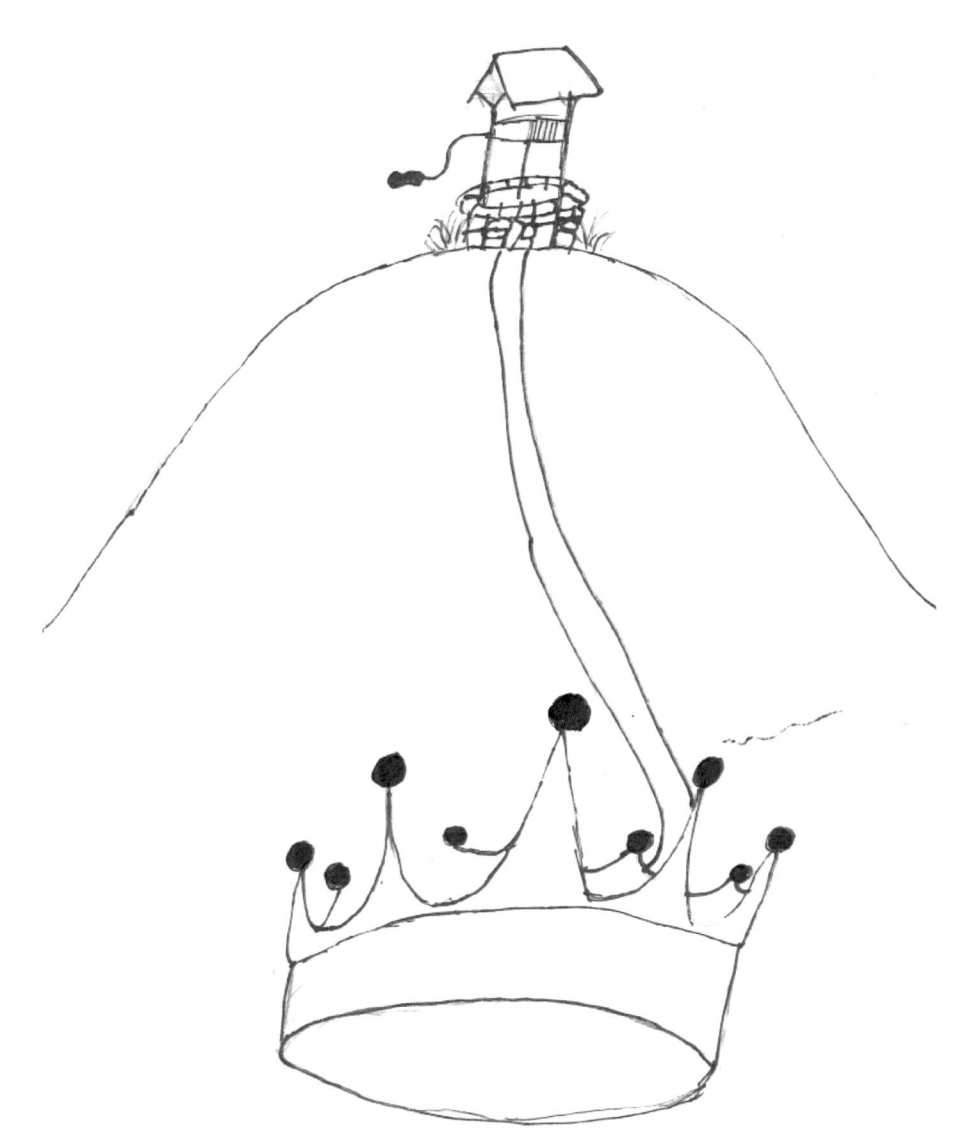

Days That Pass

Spring arrives with that snuggling
tone that hugs
the flowers and their friends
with love and the singing

of sparrows in the trees.
They make a glorious harmony,
flowering trees everywhere
with an unparalleled brightness.

Summer is approaching.
People rest on the beach to celebrate
beautiful sunrises in the afternoons
and dream in a cozy climate at night.

Autumn is approaching,
and the flowers on the trees turn into
picturesque colors,
and each leaf that falls
makes a blanket where the children begin to play.

Autumn approaches and makes the world colorful
with flowers of many colors.
Every time, they go out to rejoice
because the season will arrive with their vibrant petals
that fall together to form a cuddly blanket where animals rest.
My life is colorful thanks to it.

After that, winter arrives.
How happy I feel
as the clouds adorn my house with a white cape.
Every time I walk, I leave footprints on the ground,
and with this cape, I play.
I enjoy this day.
Snowflakes fall every day... How beautiful it is!

Ana Avellanada Acuna

The Collaborators

Mx. Hirsh has been an educator for thirteen years and is consistently wowed and inspired by their scholars. With the goal of making education fun while encouraging life-long learning, " Hirsh" or " Hirshy Bar"(as scholars refer to them) enjoys creatively thinking outside the box. Pursuing their love for creating a community that is inclusive, Hirsh weaves the intersectionality of literacy and equity into daily learning. As Hirsh tells their scholars, " your voice matters and you deserve a safe space to be heard." This anthology of poems from the heart, titled " Our Life in Poetry" blends Hirsh's love for education and the scholar's innate passion for expanding their knowledge and their minds.

Ms. Mali is a passionate art educator dedicated to nurturing creativity and self-expression in students. She believes in the transformative power of art to communicate and inspire. Mali finds joy in witnessing students' unique experiences and ideas come to life through their artwork. She particularly cherishes seeing students' confidence in their artistic abilities grow as they explore different mediums and techniques. Committed to fostering a supportive and inclusive learning environment, Mali hopes to empower these young artists to explore their creativity while emphasizing self expression and personal growth.

www.ingramcontent.com/pod-product-compliance
Lightning Source LLC
Chambersburg PA
CBRC091722070526
44585CB00007B/148